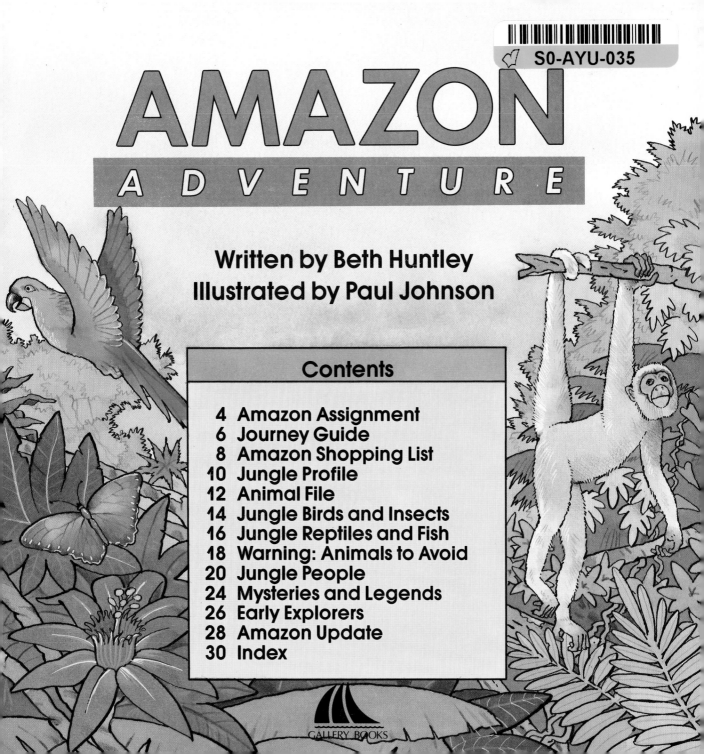

AMAZON
ADVENTURE

Written by Beth Huntley
Illustrated by Paul Johnson

Contents

GALLERY BOOKS

The Amazon is the second longest river in the world, after the Nile. It flows across the continent of South America, from the Andes mountain range to the Atlantic Ocean. Thousands of smaller rivers flow into the Amazon, and between them they drain a massive area of land covering over two million sq. miles. This area is the Amazon Basin, a huge wilderness of tropical forest and grassy plains.

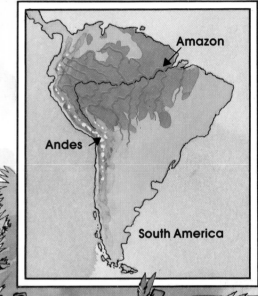

Indians have lived in the Amazon for thousands of years but Europeans only arrived in 1499, when an Italian merchant called Amerigo Vespucci took a Spanish expedition of four ships to explore the newly-discovered American continent, the "New World."

Far out from land, the explorers lowered buckets into the sea and were surprised that the water they drew up was fresh, not salty. They sailed toward the coast and to their amazement discovered the Amazon. It carries two-thirds of the world's fresh water, which flows from its mouth at over 3 billion gallons a second. The fresh water pushes aside sea water and stretches for over 99 miles into the ocean.

The Amazon is one of the richest wildlife areas in the world, but all its jungle creatures depend on a "food chain" for survival. Insects and small animals rely on jungle plants for food, and these small creatures are in turn eaten by larger ones. If the food chain is destroyed, for instance by humans destroying the forest plants, all the jungle creatures suffer.

The whole of the Amazon jungle is now threatened with destruction. You can find out more on page 28.

When the first Europeans arrived they exploited and killed the Indians, stealing their land and forcing them into slavery.

Indian land is still being stolen, even today. Now there are very few tribes left, and their ancient and unique skills are dying out.

Before it is too late we need to learn from the Indians about jungle life, and find ways of helping them to survive. You can find out more about them on page 20.

The Amazon was given its name by European explorers, after a tribe of fierce women called Amazons. Whether this tribe really existed is one of the many mysteries of the jungle. You can find out about some of them on page 24, and about early Amazon explorers on page 26.

JOURNEY GUIDE

The Amazon is over 4000 miles long and up to 2000 miles wide. It drains half the vast continent of South America, a larger expanse of land than any other river on Earth. If you were planning an Amazon expedition you would first need to decide where you wanted to visit — since the Amazon covers such a huge and varied area.

There is no single source for the river. Instead it captures water from hundreds of streams and lakes, 15,000 feet high in the cold Andes mountains.

The Amazon begins only 100 miles from the Pacific Ocean, but it travels eastwards across the continent instead of taking the quick route and flowing down the steep western slopes.

As the river gathers more water it begins to flow faster. It tumbles down the rough mountainsides in torrents and waterfalls, crashing down the valleys and taking huge boulders with it in a rush of white, foaming water.

Only a few fish can survive the pounding of the water and the rocks in this stretch of water, and a boat journey would be impossible.

Manaus

As the river reaches level jungl it slows down. By this time it is carrying huge amounts of mud wrenched from mountain ravines and ridges.

Halfway along its length it reaches Manaus, the biggest city in the Amazon region. It ha a busy riverside filled with boat

Near Manaus the Amazon is joined by another huge river, the Rio Negro, which has clear water. For some distance the two rivers flow alongside each other between the same bank but amazingly their waters never mix, so it is easy to tell the two apart.

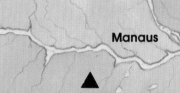

In the lowland areas of the Amazon Basin it is hot and humid, with daily rain. Over 50 inches falls each year.

At times the river bursts its banks and flood water spills out over thousands of miles into the jungle, sometimes to a depth of up to 40 feet or so.

When the jungle trees are standing in water, fish swim amongst them looking for food (see page 17), and you can paddle a boat between the trunks.

The Amazon provides the best route into the jungle. It is navigable by ocean-going ships for about 2300 miles from its mouth.

After that the best way to travel is by smaller boat. For centuries the Amazon Indians have used the perfect river craft, a lightweight canoe hollowed from a log.

Any expeditions traveling along the river need to employ some experienced navigators and jungle guides to help them in their journey.

Belém

At the end of its course, nearly 4000 miles from its tumbling beginnings, the Amazon drops its load of mud and silt to form a group of islands in mid-stream. This area is called a delta.

The Amazon has the biggest delta in the world; one of the islands is as big as the country of Switzerland!

Where the Amazon meets the Atlantic it measures a vast 200 miles from one bank to the other. At the mouth there is a port, called Belém, which handles all the boats that sail onwards up the river.

AMAZON SHOPPING LIST

Gathering together the right equipment is the most important preparation for an Amazon jungle adventure. These pages show vital explorers' equipment you need to take with you.

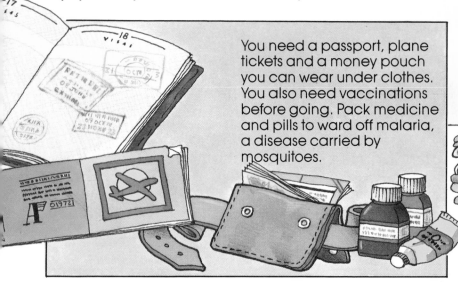

You need a passport, plane tickets and a money pouch you can wear under clothes. You also need vaccinations before going. Pack medicine and pills to ward off malaria, a disease carried by mosquitoes.

Locally-made hammocks are ideal for sleeping in, and you can fit a waterproof sleeping bag inside. You must also have mosquito nets tucked around you. Take bug repellent spray and cream to rub on any bites.

You could take a lightweight waterproof tent. Or you could sleep out in the open under a tarpaulin canopy.

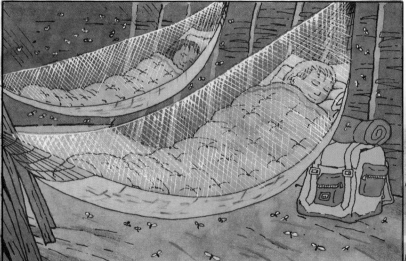

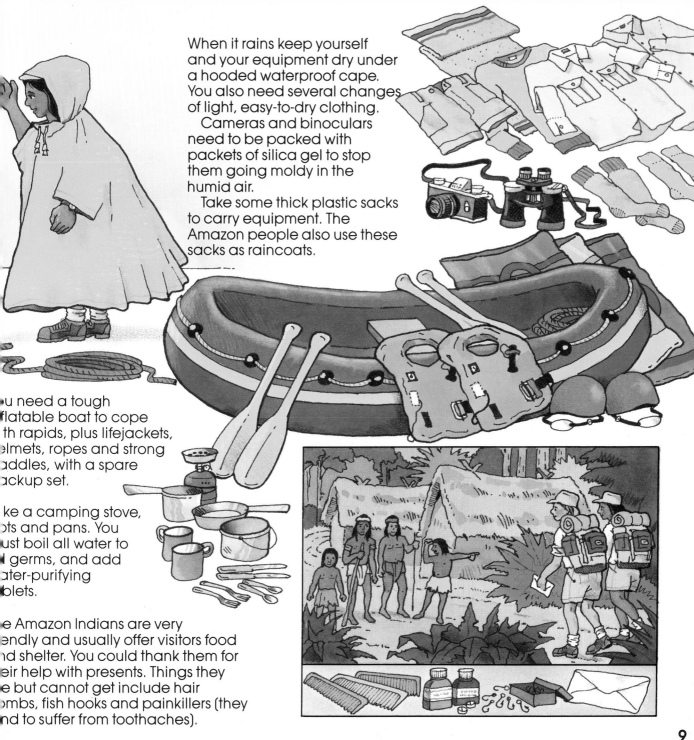

When it rains keep yourself and your equipment dry under a hooded waterproof cape. You also need several changes of light, easy-to-dry clothing.

Cameras and binoculars need to be packed with packets of silica gel to stop them going moldy in the humid air.

Take some thick plastic sacks to carry equipment. The Amazon people also use these sacks as raincoats.

You need a tough inflatable boat to cope with rapids, plus lifejackets, helmets, ropes and strong paddles, with a spare backup set.

Take a camping stove, pots and pans. You must boil all water to kill germs, and add water-purifying tablets.

The Amazon Indians are very friendly and usually offer visitors food and shelter. You could thank them for their help with presents. Things they like but cannot get include hair combs, fish hooks and painkillers (they tend to suffer from toothaches).

JUNGLE PROFILE

From the air the Amazon jungle looks like a huge mass of similar-looking green trees; but it is really made up of hundreds of varying types with lots of different animals living among the foliage.

A good way to explore jungle life would be to climb a rope ladder to the highest branch of the tallest tree – that's about 200 feet high.

On the way up you would see that wildlife varies in different layers of the tree foliage, with special groups of creatures and plants living on different levels.

A thick layer of wet leaves makes the jungle floor soft and slippery. This "leaf litter" makes a good home for thousands of insects.

The soil layer is thin, so the trees spread roots along the ground and grow supporting "buttress" roots around their trunks. Indians kick these hollow roots to make a loud booming noise. They send messages this way, rather like beating drums.

200 ft.

At this height you will find yourself in an "emergent," the name given to extra-tall trees which stick out above the rest. Harpy eagles use them as nesting sites and lookout posts (see p. 14).

115 ft.

At this level you can feel the sun and the breeze. Green rope-like plants, called lianas, hang down, and animals climb up and down them. At flowering times this layer will be a mass of brightly colored blossoms, with bees and hummingbirds busily flying around collecting nectar.

60–115 ft.

At this level you will pass many plants twined around tree branches. These plants have "aerial" roots that gather nutrients by just hanging in the air. Some have bowl-shaped leaves to catch rainwater. Monkeys sometimes scoop up the water from these natural pools.

50-60 ft.

As you look up from the ground you will see millions of leaves that form a massive green umbrella. These leaves make up the "canopy," and it is this canopy which is divided up into layers.

At 50–60 feet high you will come to a layer of branches at the top of the smallest trees. Here you may see parrots flying around, and perhaps a sloth hanging upside-down from a branch (see p. 12).

ANIMAL FILE

In the jungle it is difficult to spot animals because they are usually well-hidden by leaves. But you can often hear them; their sounds can be deafeningly loud, especially at night. A few of the many interesting Amazon animals are shown on these pages.

There are many different species of Amazon monkey. The largest is the howler monkey. It has the loudest jungle call, amplifying the sound by inflating a bag of loose skin under its chin. The call carries for miles.

Troops of little squirrel monkeys scamper along branches. The babies cling on tightly to the mothers' fur. You may also see spider monkeys. They cling on to branches with the ends of their strong tail.

At night bats use an inbuilt radar system to guide them. Amazon fruit bats also have a very strong sense of smell to help them find a ripe fruit. They grab it and cleverly twist it off its stem.

A sloth's whole life is mostly spent hanging upside-down in the trees. Sloths move very slowly, and that makes them prey for bigger animals. But green algae grows on their hairy coat and helps to camouflage them.

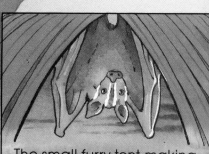

The small furry tent-making bat does not like getting wet, so it nibbles along a jungle leaf spine until both sides of the leaf flop down. When it rains the bat crawls under it.

The freshwater dolphin is a mammal that lives in the Amazon river. Unlike sea dolphins it is pink and almost blind, because the river is so muddy that good eyesight would be useless.

The dolphins are intelligent creatures. They talk to each other in a language of clicks and chirps, noises which carry clearly underwater.

Margay

...e jaguar is the biggest ...azon cat. It prowls on the ...rest floor or sits on branches ...atching for prey to pass ...eneath. Most of its hunting is ...ne in ponds and streams. ...stirs up the bottom of a pond ...th its paw to dislodge fish, or ...dangles its tail in the water as ...ait to lure them.

Ocelot.

The ocelot and the margay are both jungle cats with spotted coats which act as camouflage. They are agile climbers – the margay even has feet that turn around. It can climb down a tree trunk headfirst, while its feet still face upwards so that its claws can cling on to the bark.

JUNGLE BIRDS

In the Amazon rainforest there are many hundreds of different birds. Some of the species you might see are shown below.

The scarlet macaw is actually shaded red, yellow and blue. You may see it streaking through the jungle canopy fetching food for its young.

A careful parent will find a safe nesting hole in a tree trunk. The macaw can enlarge the natural hole with its beak and rear its chicks inside, safe from any predators who might eat the nestlings.

There are many types of jungle hummingbird. If you are lucky you might see one hovering in front of a flower, licking out the nectar. Hummingbirds beat their wings up to 79 times a second, and to get the energy to do this they must eat twice their own weight in food each day.

The hoatsin bird is thought to closely resemble prehistoric birds because for a week the newborn chicks have claws on the ends of their wings. If they fall from the nests they use the claws to climb back.

The harpy eagle i the world's largest eagle with feet the size of a man's hand! It swoops down from its high nest and grabs animals such as monkeys and sloths. The harpy itself is too big and strong for any other jungle animal to catch.

JUNGLE INSECTS

Possibly only half the world's jungle insects have so far been discovered; there are thousands in the Amazon alone. A few are shown below.

Leaf-cutter ants grow their own food, a special type of fungus. The ants bite out leaf sections and carry them back to garden areas to feed the fungus.

The colony is guarded by small ants, who stand on the leaves fighting off unfriendly insects such as flies.

Beautiful butterflies flit through the jungle canopy. Their brilliant colors make them very obvious, so to frighten off enemies some have fierce false eyes marked on their underwings, which they display when they sense danger.

Insects pollinate the many jungle flowers. One of the largest is the giant water lily, which floats on the river. At night the flower closes, trapping insects inside. The next day they escape, covered in pollen.

Stick and leaf insects have a perfect camouflage — they look just like twigs. They sit motionless amongst foliage so that their enemies cannot spot them and they can fool smaller edible insects into coming too close.

You might come across an enormous "communal web" spanning several bushes. This is spun by many spiders working together in order to trap larger prey than normal. Even hummingbirds can get tangled in the sticky silk.

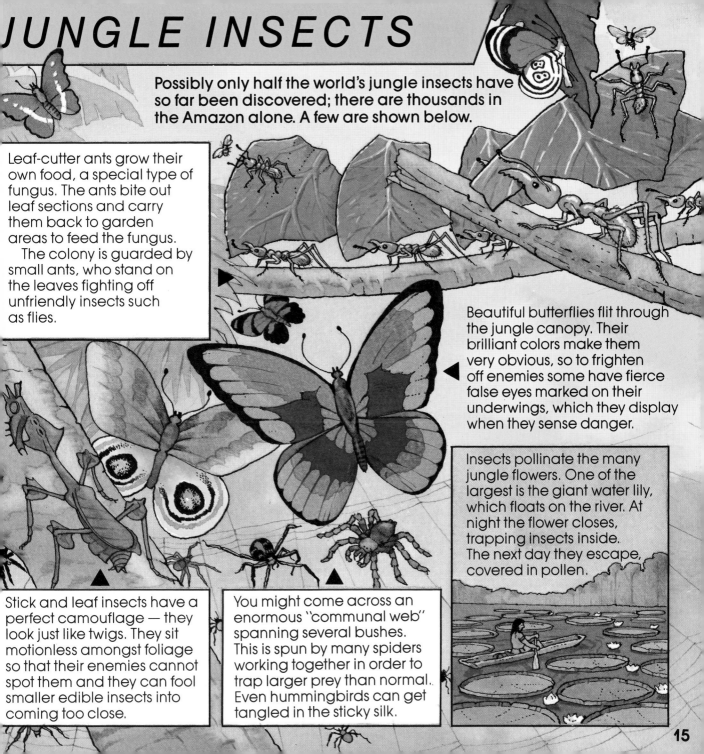

15

JUNGLE REPTILES

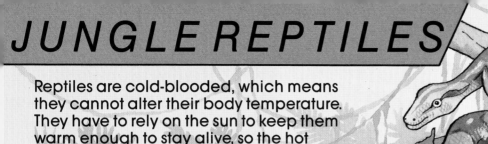

Reptiles are cold-blooded, which means they cannot alter their body temperature. They have to rely on the sun to keep them warm enough to stay alive, so the hot Amazon rainforest is ideal. Some are shown below.

There are many jungle snakes, but most are easily scared away. One of the most well-known is the boa constrictor, which can grow up to 15 feet long. It is generally harmless to humans, eating small mammals and reptiles. It can kill creatures by coiling round them and squeezing them to death.

The green tree frog is one of the many jungle frogs which you can hear calling at night. Its toes have sticky discs on the end, which help it to climb well. It eats insects, leaping high into the air to catch them.

One small riverside lizard escapes danger by standing on its back legs and running quickly across the river-surface. This ability to walk on water has given it the name "Jesus Christ lizard."

Green iguanas can grow almost 6 feet long. They are good climbers, with powerful toes for gripping on to branches.

Despite their fierce dragon-like appearance they are easily frightened, and will often escape danger by dropping down from a branch into the river and swimming quickly away underwater, using their tails to propel themselves.

Indians and Amazon travelers often eat iguana meat, which is said to taste like chicken. But the iguanas are agile and difficult to catch.

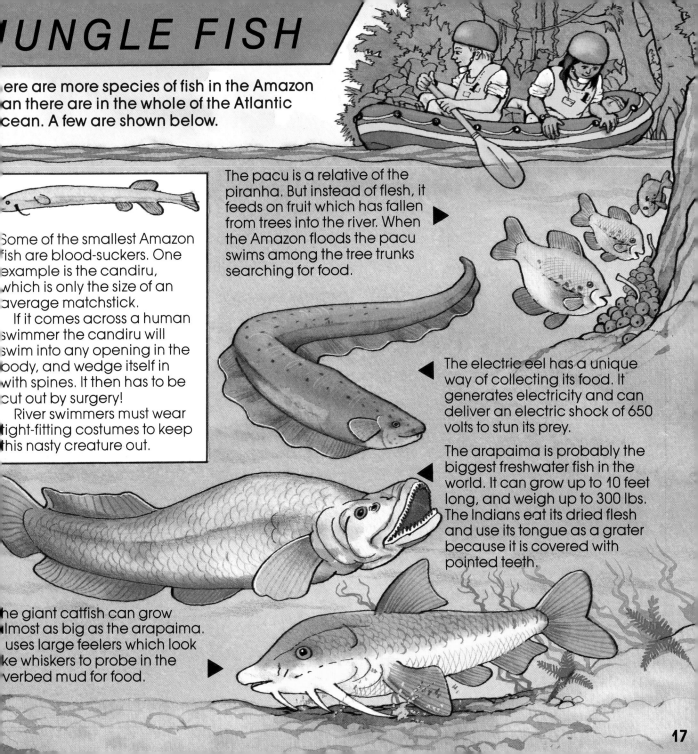

JUNGLE FISH

There are more species of fish in the Amazon than there are in the whole of the Atlantic Ocean. A few are shown below.

Some of the smallest Amazon fish are blood-suckers. One example is the candiru, which is only the size of an average matchstick.

If it comes across a human swimmer the candiru will swim into any opening in the body, and wedge itself in with spines. It then has to be cut out by surgery!

River swimmers must wear tight-fitting costumes to keep this nasty creature out.

The pacu is a relative of the piranha. But instead of flesh, it feeds on fruit which has fallen from trees into the river. When the Amazon floods the pacu swims among the tree trunks searching for food.

The electric eel has a unique way of collecting its food. It generates electricity and can deliver an electric shock of 650 volts to stun its prey.

The arapaima is probably the biggest freshwater fish in the world. It can grow up to 10 feet long, and weigh up to 300 lbs. The Indians eat its dried flesh and use its tongue as a grater because it is covered with pointed teeth.

The giant catfish can grow almost as big as the arapaima. It uses large feelers which look like whiskers to probe in the riverbed mud for food.

WARNING: ANIMALS TO AVOID

IN THE WATER

When you are traveling on the Amazon river you need to keep a sharp eye out for dangerous animals in the water, lurking ready to attack. You need to keep a special watch for the species shown below, and avoid them at all costs.

The anaconda is the heaviest snake in the world. It can grow as long as 30 feet and weigh as much as 330 lbs.

The snake's body is too heavy for it to drag over land, so it lies at the water's edge waiting to ambush prey, which it squeezes to death in its coils.

Keep a look out for sting rays if you step out of your boat onto a sandy part of the river bed. The rays have flat bodies and hide in the sand. If a ray stings you, you need to put something hot on the sting to draw the poison out.

If you see a rotten log floating in the river, watch out; it could be a crocodile! The Amazon crocodile is called the cayman, and grows up to 15 feet long. It can move with lightning speed and will lie in wait to attack any land animal that it sees coming close to the edge of the water.

Piranhas are small fish but some species can be deadly. They hunt in shoals and will attack anything that makes a commotion in the water.

Piranha teeth are so sharp that they can tear an animal to pieces in minutes. Amazonian Indians use the teeth as scissors.

ON LAND

Most Amazonian land animals are shy and will only attack if disturbed. But snakes and spiders tend to lurk hidden on the forest floor, so you need to watch where you put your feet. Avoid the animals shown below. They can be deadly.

Always make sure your mosquito net is well tucked in, because Amazonian vampire bats will land on sleeping animals and suck blood from exposed parts of the body. This is not fatal itself, but the bats can pass on the deadly rabies disease.

The bushmaster snake is particularly hard to see against jungle foliage because it has camouflaged brown skin. Its bite can kill you in hours.

This snake spots its prey by sensing body-heat, using heat-seekers on each side of its head. It can grow up to 10 feet long.

The tiny blue and red arrow poison frog makes the strongest poison produced by an animal. It squeezes the poison from its skin, and the smallest amount can kill a human. Amazonian Indians sometimes use the poison on the tips of their arrows.

Tarantulas are among the biggest spiders in the world, and they can grow as big as a man's fist. They usually feed on small reptiles, beetles and birds.

Humans bitten by these spiders fall very ill, although the poison is not usually fatal to people.

Scorpions like to creep into dark holes and warm places, so you need to watch out for them in equipment, especially in boots and bags. They can give you a nasty sting with their tails. This is not fatal but it is quite painful for a few days.

19

JUNGLE PEOPLE

Before the Europeans arrived in South America in the 1500s there were about ten million Amazon Indians living in up to 700 separate tribes. Each tribe had its own land and customs.

Since that time the lives of the Indians have changed completely, and their ancient skills are quickly dying out. There are now only a few hundred thousand left.

The remaining Indian tribes live in small communities in jungle clearings. Lots of relatives usually live in one large "communal" house built from jungle branches and palm leaves.

The tribes organize themselves in different ways. For instance, in some tribes there is a head man and a ruling council, whereas in other tribes every member has equal rights and all possessions are shared.

The Jivaro Indians of Peru and Equador are one example of a surviving rainforest tribe.

In the past the Jivaro were very warlike, and as part of their rituals they would shrink the heads of the enemies they killed in battle.

Nowadays the Jivaro only shrink the heads of animals they have hunted, such as sloths and monkeys.

The Indians remove the skin of the animal and shrink it by soaking it in a mixture of jungle tree bark and water.

Then the skin is stuffed to make it look like a perfect miniature head, only a few inches high.

The Jivaro hang the heads outside their huts, partly because it shows their bravery and prowess in hunting.

The Waorani tribe from Equador are particularly skilled at hunting animals. They use a blowpipe, a straight hollow piece of wood about 10 feet long. It fires slender wooden darts tipped with a strong poison called curare, made from the bark of a vine.

If the hunter kills something small, such as a monkey, he will carry it home hanging from his shoulder. But it takes two people to carry a wild pig, hung beneath a branch. When the hunter arrives home the meat is chopped up, cooked and shared.

When a hunter spots an animal he puts a dart in the end of the pipe, with a wedge of woolly material called kapok rolled round it. Then he takes aim by raising the heavy blowpipe (which can weigh up to 10 lbs.). With one sharp puff the dart can travel up to 1000 feet.

Manioc

The Indians know where to look for edible plants in the jungle, and they also grow their own vegetables.

One of the most popular plants to grow is manioc, which looks like a long, thin potato. It is made into a drink by peeling, boiling, and mashing. Then it is mixed with water and saliva. It is left to ferment so it becomes slightly alcoholic.

The Indians usually have the manioc drink at breakfast and at bedtime, often when they are lying in their hammocks listening to ancient tales. They usually offer the drink to visitors.

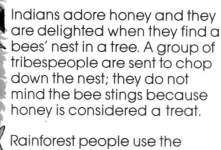

Indians adore honey and they are delighted when they find a bees' nest in a tree. A group of tribespeople are sent to chop down the nest; they do not mind the bee stings because honey is considered a treat.

Rainforest people use the jungle trees in other ways. They roll palm fiber into string and weave it into hammocks, and use tree bark to make comfortable baby slings.

The Indians often plant chonta fruit trees in their jungle gardens. The chonta fruit looks rather like a red peach, and it has a pleasant chestnut flavor when it is boiled.

The tree trunk is covered in spines, so the Indians plant a smooth-trunked cecropia tree next to each chonta. They can climb this and reach across for the chonta fruit.

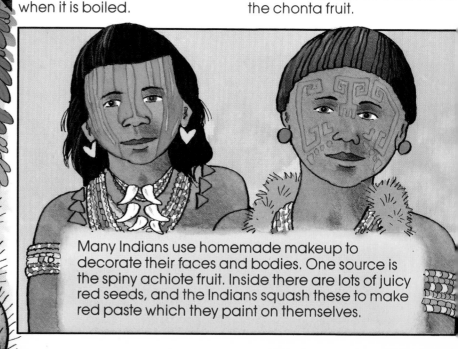

Many Indians use homemade makeup to decorate their faces and bodies. One source is the spiny achiote fruit. Inside there are lots of juicy red seeds, and the Indians squash these to make red paste which they paint on themselves.

Some Indians are very good fishermen. One easy way to catch fish is to make a fish poison by crushing the leaves of the barbasco plant to produce a milky paste. When this is poured into the water it kills small fish and stuns larger ones. The fishermen wade in to collect them.

Since the Amazon was first discovered international companies have mined its minerals and have cleared vast jungle areas for the wood.

Many Indian tribes have lost their homes and land. They are treated as children in law, and so they cannot fight for their land through the courts.

A major problem is that the Indians have very little resistance to illnesses brought in by outsiders. These spread as deadly epidemics, and have wiped out many tribes.

International projects have now been organized to try to help the Indians survive. You can find out more on page 29.

MYSTERIES AND LEGENDS

In the Amazon region there are still mysteries for explorers to solve. For instance, there are many strange stories of monsters, treasure hoards and lost explorers. The truth behind many of these stories may never be known. Here are some of them.

In 1920, an Amazon explorer saw two huge monkeys, screaming and brandishing tree branches. They could not have been gorillas, because there are no gorillas in South America. Other travelers have seen giant apes in the jungle, but no one has photographed or captured one.

El Dorado, the City of Gold, is still the greatest mystery of the Amazon. It is said that El Dorado ("the golden man"), was the king of this city. He was so rich he covered himself in gold dust.

Once a year the king was said to swim in a lake high in the mountains. The gold dust was washed off, and the Indians threw gold and jewels after it. This treasure still lies hidden, though many have searched for it.

Somewhere in the jungle, there is supposed to be a great ruined city. In 1925 the explorer Percy Fawcett set out with two friends to find the ruins. They were never seen again.

Nobody knows what happened to Fawcett. Some say he was killed by Indians. Others say he lived the rest of his life in an Indian village.

The Indians of the Amazon believe in many ghosts and monsters. The most frightening of these is the Mapinguari, who is said to have one eye in the middle of his forehead.

This monster is also said to have no feet, and a body covered in hair. His scream is supposed to be so loud and strong that it can knock a human over with its force.

Many strange tales have been told about mythical Amazonian tribes. Some are told by local Indians, others by early explorers who made up fantastic stories about what they saw. Some of these mythical tribes are listed below:
—a tribe of one-legged people.
—a tribe who whistle through holes in their heads.
—a tribe of bat people who come out at night.
—a tribe who are half-man and half-fish.

One Amazon legend tells of a gentle jungle monster called the Caipora, whose feet are turned back to front. He is supposed to look after the jungle animals and heal them when they are wounded.

Any hunter who kills too many animals will be punished by the Caipora. He will lay false tracks so that the hunter gets hopelessly lost.

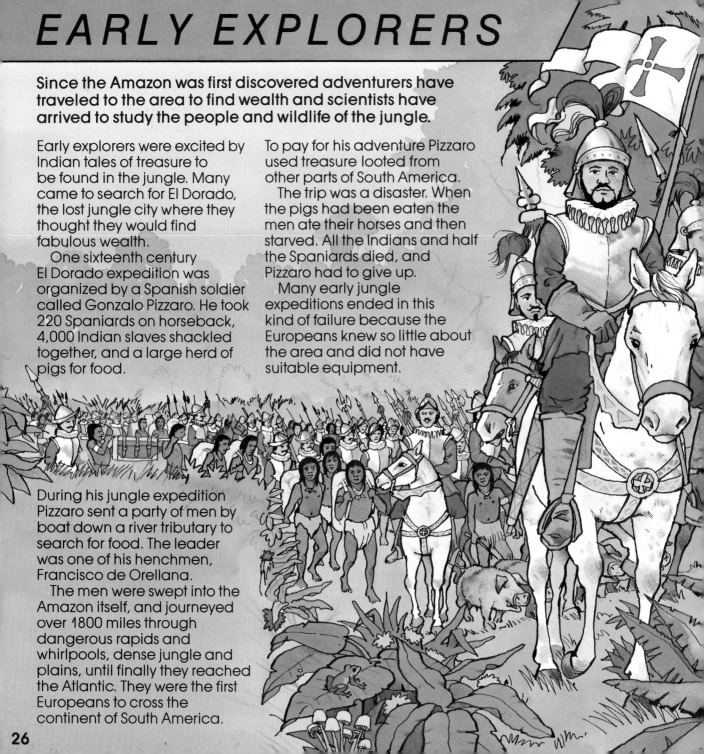

EARLY EXPLORERS

Since the Amazon was first discovered adventurers have traveled to the area to find wealth and scientists have arrived to study the people and wildlife of the jungle.

Early explorers were excited by Indian tales of treasure to be found in the jungle. Many came to search for El Dorado, the lost jungle city where they thought they would find fabulous wealth.

One sixteenth century El Dorado expedition was organized by a Spanish soldier called Gonzalo Pizzaro. He took 220 Spaniards on horseback, 4,000 Indian slaves shackled together, and a large herd of pigs for food.

To pay for his adventure Pizzaro used treasure looted from other parts of South America.

The trip was a disaster. When the pigs had been eaten the men ate their horses and then starved. All the Indians and half the Spaniards died, and Pizzaro had to give up.

Many early jungle expeditions ended in this kind of failure because the Europeans knew so little about the area and did not have suitable equipment.

During his jungle expedition Pizzaro sent a party of men by boat down a river tributary to search for food. The leader was one of his henchmen, Francisco de Orellana.

The men were swept into the Amazon itself, and journeyed over 1800 miles through dangerous rapids and whirlpools, dense jungle and plains, until finally they reached the Atlantic. They were the first Europeans to cross the continent of South America.

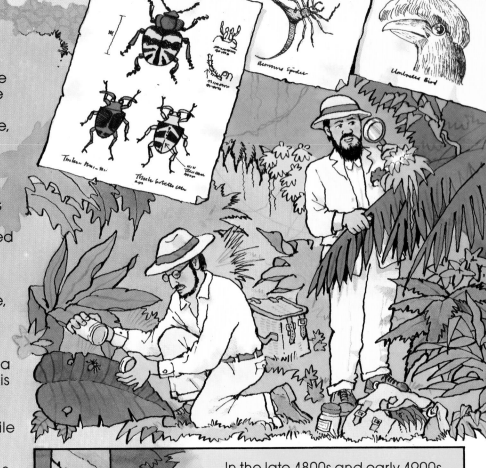

In the 1800s scientists began to come to the Amazon to study the wildlife and people. Three of the earliest visitors were the British naturalists, Alfred Russel Wallace, Henry Walter Bates and Richard Spruce, who took his dog Sultan on his travels.

These explorers spent years collecting and drawing species that had never been seen by scientists before. They contributed a great deal to our present-day knowledge of the jungle.

Each man had some hair-raising experience. For example, Wallace caught malaria on his journey and was cared for by Indians who had never seen a white man before. He once met a jaguar on a jungle path when his gun was loaded with useless birdshot. Fortunately the jaguar only looked at Wallace for a while and then strolled on.

One famous visitor was former U.S. President Theodore Roosevelt. His party canoed down an unmapped Amazon tributary in 1914.

It was a difficult journey, through many rapids and whirlpools. Roosevelt became ill and some of his Indian guides were killed on the way.

In the late 1800s and early 1900s Europeans flocked to the Amazon to make their fortunes from rubber. Millions of rubber trees were tapped for their sap, and in the process many Indians were taken as slaves.

The Brazilian government made it illegal to export the rubber trees, but eventually some were smuggled out and sent to south-east Asia. The rubber business soon flourished there, and this caused the Amazon trade to die.

27

AMAZON UPDATE

The Amazon jungle is neither as glorious nor as massive as it was when the early travelers arrived. Humans are rapidly destroying it, so the next few years may be your last chance to visit it before it is altered forever.

The Amazon Indians are being gradually driven from their old way of life. Their lands have been dug up for mines, cleared of trees or flooded by dams built for hydroelectric schemes. When these dams are built vast areas of the jungle are flooded to create large lakes, and all the animals who live there are drowned. Conservationists argue that there is already sufficient electricity in some of the areas where dams are planned, so further flooding is not necessary.

Millions of animals are killed when the jungle trees are chopped down. Creatures such as parrots, jaguars and monkeys cannot survive without their jungle homes, and some species are disappearing. For instance, expeditions in the next few years may be the last to see the woolly monkey, and some of the Amazon's most beautiful parrots.

Many trees are cut down in order to reach a particularly valuable tree, the mahogany, which is used to make fine furniture. The trees surrounding the mahogany are chopped down and just left to rot.

The Amazon forest is gradually being felled, at a rate of over 20 million acres every year: that's nearly 100 sq. miles a day. It is irreplaceable.

Although some tribes still live in the forest many Indians now live only in Indian reserves, a fraction of the size of their original land. They are gradually forgetting the skills that once enabled them to live in harmony with the jungle.

International organizations are trying to help the remaining forest tribes by campaigning to get areas of land set aside for them.

It is important that the Amazon Indians survive and that we learn from them. They alone know the secrets of living in the rainforest, and they alone can teach us their unique skills and knowledge of wildlife.

29

INDEX

If you would like to know more about the Amazon Indians you can contact the address shown below:

Amazon Conservation Foundation
18328 Gulf Boulevard
Indian Shores, FL 34625

National Geographic Society
17th and M Streets NW
Washington D.C. 20036